Chugs

by Ruth Owen

PowerKiDS
press

New York

Published in 2015 by The Rosen Publishing Group, Inc.
29 East 21st Street, New York, NY 10010

First Edition

Produced for Rosen by Ruby Tuesday Books Ltd
Editor for Ruby Tuesday Books Ltd: Mark J. Sachner
US Editor: Joshua Shadowens
Designer: Emma Randall

Photo Credits:
Cover, 1, 3, 4–5, 6–7, 8–9, 11, 12–13, 15, 16–17, 20–21, 24, 28–29, 30 ©
Shutterstock; 10, 14 © Public domain; 18–19, 26–27 © Warren Photographic;
25 © Alamy.

Library of Congress Cataloging-in-Publication Data

Owen, Ruth, 1967– author.
 Chugs / by Ruth Owen. — First edition.
    pages cm. — (Designer dogs)
 Includes index.
 ISBN 978-1-4777-7047-4 (library binding) — ISBN 978-1-4777-7048-1 (pbk.) —
 ISBN 978-1-4777-7049-8 (6-pack)
1. Chug—Juvenile literature. 2. Toy dogs—Juvenile literature. 3. Dogs—
Juvenile literature. I. Title.
 SF429.C48O84 2015
 636.76—dc23
                        2014006033

Manufactured in the United States of America

CPSIA Compliance Information: Batch #WS14PK8: For Further Information contact Rosen Publishing, New York, New York at 1-800-237-9932

Contents

Meet a Chug

What has short, glossy hair, big brown eyes, is cute and friendly, and wants to spend hours curled up in your lap? The answer is a chug.

Chugs are a **crossbreed** dog. This means they are a mixture of two different dog **breeds**. When a Chihuahua and a pug have puppies together, they make chugs.

A chug may look and act more like a Chihuahua or more like a pug. The little dog may also be a mixture of both its parents' looks and personalities.

Adult Chihuahua   Adult pug   Chug puppy

The name "chug" is made up from the names "Chihuahua" and "pug". These dogs are also sometimes called pugwawas.

This adult chug looks more like its Chihuahua parent.

5

Dogs Big and Small

The American Kennel Club's official list of dog breeds includes over 175 different breeds. Each of these dog breeds was created by people.

About 14,000 years ago, people began to train wolves and other wild dogs to be **tame**. Over many years, people **mated** different types of dogs together to create working dogs, pet dogs, big dogs, and tiny dogs.

The giant Great Dane was originally bred for hunting wild boars. Tiny Chihuahuas were pet dogs bred to live as **companions** to people.

A chug puppy

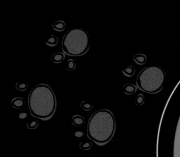

In the past 20 to 30 years, dog breeders have created some new types of dogs. These dogs, such as chugs, are known as designer dogs. That's because they were designed, or created, from existing dog breeds.

A Great Dane

A Chihuahua

Meet the Parents: Chihuahuas

The Chihuahua is the smallest dog breed in the world. A fully grown adult Chihuahua usually weighs less than 6 pounds (2.7 kg).

Tiny Chihuahuas have huge personalities, though. They are confident, **self-important** dogs that have no idea they are smaller than most of their doggie pals!

Chihuahuas make smart, loving, friendly pets. They are happy to cuddle on their owners' laps. They are even known as "purse dogs" because they are happy to ride in their owners' purses!

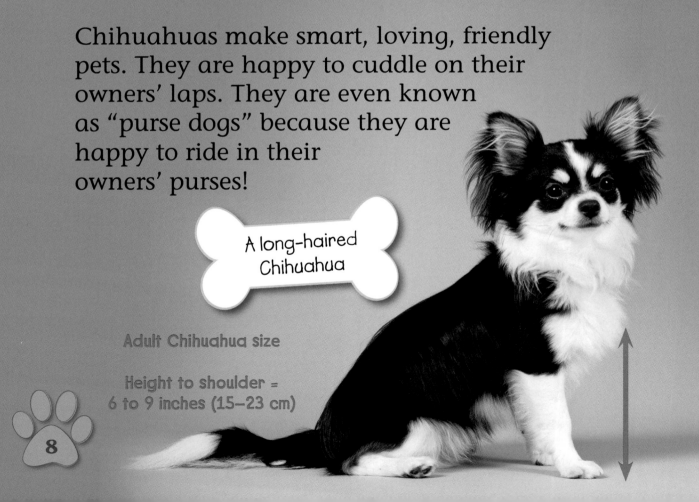

A long-haired Chihuahua

Adult Chihuahua size

Height to shoulder = 6 to 9 inches (15–23 cm)

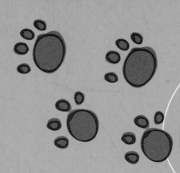

A Chihuahua can have a short or long coat. Chihuahuas come in many colors, including black, many shades of brown, cream, white, and gray. Some are even spotted.

Three Chihuahuas in a travel purse

A spotted Chihuahua

9

Meet the Parents: Chihuahua History

No one knows for sure how the Chihuahua breed got started. There are two main **theories**, however.

One theory is that the **ancestors** of the Chihuahua were Techichi dogs. These dogs lived in Mexico. The Techichi were companions to ancient peoples, including the Toltecs who lived in Mexico about 1,000 years ago.

The other theory is that, hundreds of years ago, people brought Chinese crested dogs from China to Mexico. These dogs mated with local dogs, and the Chihuahua was created.

An ancient pottery statue of a Techichi dog

A Chinese crested dog

One thing that is known about Chihuahuas is that the breed came into being in Mexico. The breed is named after the Mexican state of Chihuahua.

A Chihuahua

Meet the Parents: Pugs

Like Chihuahuas, little pugs have huge personalities. They are smart, cheerful, playful dogs that love to clown around. They give their owners lots of love and need to be with them as much as possible. If a pug is left home alone too often, it will become unhappy.

A pug has a large, round, wrinkled face with a short, flat-looking muzzle. It has a solid, rectangular body and a tightly curled tail. An adult pug can weigh up to 20 pounds (9 kg).

A pug's short, glossy coat can be black, fawn, silver, or an apricot color.

Adult pug size

Height = about 12 inches (30 cm) to the shoulder

A black pug puppy

Meet the Parents: Royal Pugs

Pugs are an ancient dog breed. Over 2,400 years ago in China, pugs lived in royal palaces as the precious companions of emperors and empresses.

In the 1500s and 1600s, traders took pugs from China to Europe. The little dogs soon became popular with wealthy Europeans and Europe's royal families. As a young woman, Queen Marie Antoinette of France had a pug. So did Napoleon's wife, the Empress Josephine. In the 1800s, Britain's Queen Victoria became a fan of the little wrinkled pups.

Pugs have appeared in many paintings from history.

A Dutch prince, William of Orange, was saved from murderers by his pug, Pompey. The prince was asleep in his tent near a battlefield. As the murderers got close, Pompey jumped onto the sleeping prince, woke him, and warned him of the danger.

A pug

15

Chug Puppies

A **litter** of chug puppies may have a pug mother and a Chihuahua father. Some litters have a Chihuahua mom and pug dad.

The mother dog may give birth to up to eight chug puppies at one time. Sometimes, however, the litter is smaller.

Like all young puppies, the little chugs feed on milk from their mom. By the time the pups are four weeks old, they are ready to eat canned puppy food, too. The pups' diet of milk and puppy food gives them lots of energy for play-fighting and running around.

A chug puppy must stay with its mother for the first eight to 10 weeks. Then the pup is big enough and strong enough to leave its mom and go to live with a new human family.

A Chug's Looks

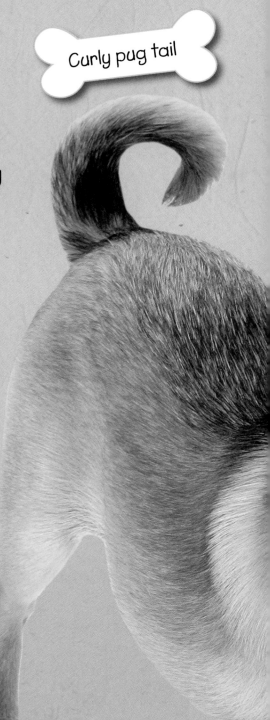

Curly pug tail

Some chugs are tiny like their Chihuahua parent, while others are larger and take after their pug mom or dad. A fully grown chug can weigh between 10 and 20 pounds (4.5–9 kg).

A chug may have a muzzle, like its Chihuahua parent, and wrinkles on its face, like its pug mother or father. Its hair may be fawn, tan, black, or any of the colors that pugs and Chihuahuas come in.

A fawn and black coat from either parent

18

A chug usually has a coat of short, smooth hair. If its Chihuahua parent, or a Chihuahua ancestor, had long hair, however, a chug's coat may grow longer.

Chihuahua ears

Pug wrinkles and Chihuahua muzzle

A Chug's Beauty Routine

A chug may shed, or lose, quite a lot of hair around the house. Shedding is something that a chug mostly **inherits** from its pug parent.

To remove the loose hair from a chug's coat, brush his or her hair every day with a special dog brush. This will make the chug's coat shiny. It will also keep lots of hair from collecting on the furniture and carpets.

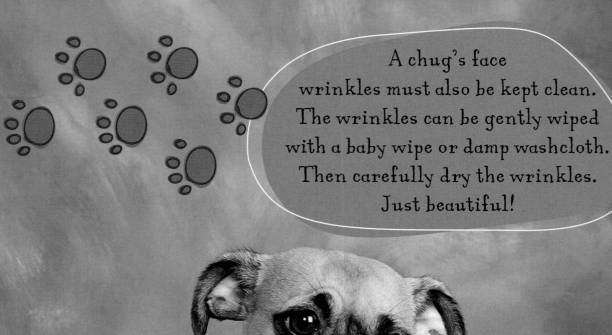

A chug's face wrinkles must also be kept clean. The wrinkles can be gently wiped with a baby wipe or damp washcloth. Then carefully dry the wrinkles. Just beautiful!

21

Chug Personalities

Just like its looks, a chug's personality may be more like one parent than the other. Hopefully, a chug will be a mixture of both its parents' best qualities.

For example, Chihuahuas can sometimes be unsure around strangers. Pugs, however, are more laid back. Pugs can sometimes be stubborn, whereas Chihuahuas are good at obeying orders. A chug that inherits the best parts of its parents' personalities will hopefully turn out to be friendly to new people and easy to manage and train.

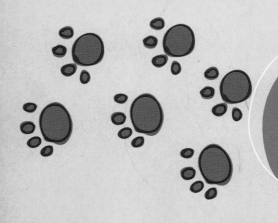

Chugs take their job as a companion very seriously. They love to be with their owners and have heaps of love to give.

Living With a Chug

A chug will be happy living in a home with a backyard or in a small apartment.

Like their pug relatives, chugs often like to eat—a lot! It's important, therefore, that a chug gets daily exercise to avoid becoming overweight. A walk around the neighborhood or an energetic play session each day will keep a chug in shape.

Like their parents, chugs are smart and they learn fast. If they receive lots of praise and food rewards, they will quickly learn new tricks.

Learning new tricks is fun!

A trip to the park is fun, too!

Chugs often paw at and burrow under covers and pillows. They get this habit from their Chihuahua relatives.

Chug Talk

Everyone knows that when a dog wags its tail, it's happy. There are many different ways, however, that chugs and other dogs "talk" to each other and their owners by using their bodies.

If you tell your chug off, it may crouch low to the ground and lay its ears flat. The little pup is showing you that it knows you're the boss.

If a chug puts one of its front legs around another dog's shoulder, it's saying "play with me."

A chug and its pug best friend

Like its Chihuahua parent, a chug may not know its own size. It might try to start a fight with a much bigger dog. It's important, therefore, to carefully introduce a young chug to lots of other dogs so it learns good puppy manners. It must learn that it's not OK to start doggie trouble.

27

Most Valuable Puppy

While some people choose to watch the Super Bowl, for millions, the big sports event of Super Bowl Sunday is *Animal Planet's Puppy Bowl.*

Dozens of adorable pups try to score touchdowns with chew toys in a miniature football stadium. The puppies that take part are all from rescue shelters and are waiting to find new forever homes. During the game, penalties may be called for napping, howling, or peeing on the field!

Every year, fans of the show can vote for the MVP—Most Valuable Puppy. At Puppy Bowl VI in 2010, a chug named Jake was voted MVP!

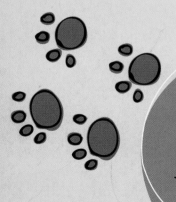

Over several days, film crews tape hours of puppy play in the mini football stadium. Then the best shots are combined to create the *Puppy Bowl* show and make it look as if the pups are really playing football.

Glossary

ancestors (AN-ses-terz) Relatives who lived long ago.

breeds (BREEDZ) Different types of dogs. The word "breed" is also used to describe the act of mating two dogs in order for them to have puppies.

companions (kum-PAN-yunz) People or animals with whom one spends a lot of time.

crossbreed (KROS-breed) A type of dog created from two different breeds.

inherits (in-HER-its) Has a quality, such as hair color or size, that has been passed on by parents and may come from ancestors, which are relatives that lived long ago.

litter (LIH-ter)
A group of baby animals all born to the same mother at the same time.

mated (MAYT-ed)
Put a male and female animal together so that they produce young.

self-important
(self-im-POR-tunt) Having a strong belief that you are more important than you actually are.

tame (TAYM)
Not dangerous, and friendly toward people.

theories
(THEE-uh-reez) Ideas or beliefs that are based on only a small amount of factual information.

Websites
Due to the changing nature of Internet links, PowerKids Press has developed an online list of websites related to the subject of this book. This site is updated regularly. Please use this link to access the list:

www.powerkidslinks.com/ddog/chug/

Read More

Burstein, John. *Dogs*. Slim Goodbody's Inside Guide to Pets. New York: Gareth Stevens, 2008.

Rockwood, Leigh. *Dogs Are Smart!* Super Smart Animals. New York: PowerKids Press, 2010.

Shores. Erika L. *All about Chihuahuas*. Dogs, Dogs, Dogs. Mankato, MN: Capstone Press, 2013.

Index